GROWING

Also by David Lindley

Poetry
How to Write a Haiku
Book of Days
Something & Nothing: Selected Poems

Philosophy
The Freedom to Be Tragic
Ideas of Order

Translations
The Way It Is: The Tao Te Ching of Lao Tzu
The Song of Myself: A new verse translation of The Bhagavad Gita

GROWING

David Lindley

Growing is the strange death
In life that nobody mourns
Elizabeth Smart

Verborum Editions

© David Lindley 2020

First published 2020 by Verborum Editions

Verborum Editions
5 Lauds Road
Crick
Northamptonshire
NN6 7TJ

www.verborumeditions.com

978-1-907100-07-9

For my sister Brenda
and
to the memory of my father

HORSE CHESTNUT

The boy
fell from the tree
and died
before he could hold
all that the heart
desires all
that was true
before it could
open before
it was new.

GROWING

Then there was nothing else
but boyhood and the blankness
of being perpetual
riding the bus
over the endless plain
of carpet pile.
No one came
and no one went
and the end
was just the same
as the beginning
always departing
and never arriving.

GROWING

A paradise
of green hills
seen from
the smoke-filled
valley.
A paradise
the smoke-filled
valley
now we are
newly housed
on a green hill.

GROWING

When things were short
or fell short
when there was not enough
of the material
she proved herself
metaphysical in this
making do
with what there is.

GROWING

The sideboard
was a sacred object
two cupboards
three drawers
each with a hidden purpose
disclosed only to one
high priestess
mysteries
that only she knew
the top and bottom of.

GROWING

Not to pick
the bluebells
not to bring home
daffodils
not to be led
into temptation
by the spring.
You can't hold on
to things for ever.
Who says?
Mam.
God.

GROWING

This year
there'll be no fireworks
the carpet is rolled up
ready to go
the lightbulb
glowers at me
from under its shade
the wrecked settee
is traumatised.
You can leave too
since you should have brought
fireworks but didn't.

GROWING

Mother nattering
father studying
he says
each with an anxious
index finger
against a forehead
full of foreboding
and forbidding.

GROWING

The steps are whitened
old woman sits for a while
mother comes out with a broom.

GROWING

Waiting
looking out
swinging
on the door chain
taste of iron
a falling out
of concepts
and categories
of self
and pavement
when my head
was at one
with the world
outside time.

GROWING

Washing on a line across the street
coal wagon delivering
the eternal conflict of light and dark.

GROWING

We were as much at home
on the streets
as pigeons
or hens laying away
mothers leaning out of windows
calling home their brood.

GROWING

Christopher in his playpen
was as territorial
as a stickleback in a jar of minnows.
Behave nicely
said the mother hen
to the wolf.

GROWING

We followed the golden cross
from the iron church
under the steel-grey sky
the wind
whipped the daffodils
shaking their heads
in disbelief.

GROWING

Usually I galloped home
on my horse
beating its rump
cloppety cloppety clop
my first dactylic line
all in my head.
When someone called out
Ride him cowboy!
I awoke and found myself
without a leg to stand on.
This was before
the invention of conversation
about nothing
one day walking home
with Margaret Smales
a game that grown-ups play
in a world of their own.

GROWING

We shared
the same recurring dream
that one day
stumbling along
at the water's edge
like that
his polio-afflicted leg
in a brace
he'd fall in.
That day came
and we watched
helplessly dreaming
for the dream
was about falling
helplessly falling
and we thought
we were dreaming.

GROWING

I tumbled
down
the grassy hill
dead
again
rising
again
a whole life
flashing
by.

GROWING

Old mulberry tree
supporting itself on a stick.
Under its shade
not even ten summers.

GROWING

Boys on the way to school
biting into crusts.
Raspberry-red smiles.

GROWING

The swimming baths
adjoined the public library.
We made our way back to school
past the slaughterhouse
carrying wet towels
black pudding and books.

GROWING

Someone is knocking
too cold to open the door.
Ah, hot pea soup man.

GROWING

The smell of coal dust
oil damp wood leather
tobacco manliness
behind the cellar door.
Ah, cellar door
Poe thought
the most beautiful words
in the English language.

GROWING

Dib-dib
dob-dob
drip-drip
drop by drop
the calcified child
building a backbone
of resistance.

GROWING

What was the ice-cream man
doing out in the snow?
Delivering a message up the hill –
she's not coming.

GROWING

It was all over
before I was born
since then
I have lived a life
of perfect crime.

GROWING

It must have been
a gypsy switch
one morning
left outside as usual
to cootchy-coo
with any passing stranger
how else explain
this unbelonging
known only
to that caravan
of lost souls
wandering the zodiac?

GROWING

I knew at once
this was a serious business
I took refuge in a child
to think about it
it seemed to be
what everybody wanted
so I hid myself
deferring my obvious absence
that no one noticed.

GROWING

I could have been
a contender
for the lightest
fightless flightiest
flyweight
but carried
a repeated note
of excuses
a note to the bell
sounding hollow.

GROWING

Love suffocates
but also exposes you
to snow-filled
wellington boots
leg irons
poultices
nit combs
shavings of green
soap up your arse
the admonition
of curtains drawn
against the coming
of night
and tomorrow.

GROWING

What are you doing?
Sitting still doing nothing
like it says in this book.
Books books books!
then she threw them
down the stairs.

GROWING

Here
bullet holes
in the wall
here
a firing range
prizes of red
paper roses.

GROWING

From then on
at the end of every day
the jaws of night
would be waiting
in every dream
at the end of every affair
the same triumphant face
of grinning dentures
where all the heroes
of the world are crushed
and there is no refuge
in the arms of love
that bear the immortal infant
out of the sun
into the night rain.

GROWING

Small betrayals
lies
no more than wishes
to be true
that greedy old man
at Christmas
what was he doing here
keeping me awake
without reason
the nurse who said
she'd telephone my mother
and I cried the more
because we had no phone
small deceits
disguising pain
and the real
in the end they betrayed
themselves
phoney accents
in front of the waiter
broken fag hanging
from the corner of a mouth
tough guy
yeah
I saw what they were doing
a conspiracy with themselves
in a mirror
I saw them in the mirror
and afterwards we never spoke again
for they'd seen me in the mirror too
and they knew
I knew mortality's intimation

GROWING

that we make it all up
and lie
only to get through
this silence.

IN THE PARK

Take, eat these crusts of bread
I saved for you, cast upon
the waters of the lake.
Sing, crows, on high
the coarse black syllables
of my song among the boughs
where my redeemer lives.
Bow down before me,
mulberry tree, leaning
on your old man's stick.
Treat me to an ice cream, Mam,
and then descend with me
from many mansions of my dreams
the stairway past the noble urns
through leafy paths and grottos
hollowed out by wind and rain
and take me in your arms
and lift me up and let me
see the world again.

SNAP TIN

I feared this
growing up
his early morning rising
buckling a gabardine
taking a hat from behind the door
and the thought
of her being there
always
dressed in a housecoat
anticipating the dust of my absence
in every corner

and the snap tin
would be on the draining board
packed up the night before
and it too at eleven exactly
would open its aluminium jaws
and mock me with the secrets
of another life
that no one speaks of

for dust has settled here
from stars that went out overnight
and there is fluff
in the lining of my pockets.

And then God came to me
as in a dream and said
I give you cheese and pickle
for you are my well-beloved.

PROMISES

Through the gate
at evening down the hill
I must have passed the space
of grassy ground not yet
the grave of fatherhood
defying him
to walk out late to meet her
where she stood
among the shadows.
Margaret was it? Grace?
I don't remember
or what was promised
but he was right to say
that time would break
all promises
when I walked down
the churchyard way
and past
that disappointed place.

LOVE LANE

Love Lane
no love here
a blank wall
the outer perimeter
of Wakefield prison.

Over the back fence
into grandad's rhubarb patch
like a thief
through the scullery window
left open.
Half a pork pie
then waiting for judgment.

Hadn't I already been judged?
This is my outer circle –
out through the clackety gate
and the privet hedge
to the bus stop
then waiting – fourpence
will pay the conductor
to take me to the inner heart of it.

A settee, flowery wallpaper
forty-watt bulb
in some sort of crepe lampshade
segmented like fish scales
then waiting – for what?

For love, for the true heart of it.

GROWING

Love, hearts –
you could buy them
in a sugary packet
on the way to school
and all might be redeemed
I'd read by faith
or with coupons
at the corner shop.

IT WAS THE FURNITURE

It was the furniture
when I think of the moment
my soul decided to leave
this body behind
as though it too could be thrown out.
I had knocked the stuffing
out of the settee
that to them bore
no resemblance to a teddy bear
with its heart torn from it
which might have lent it
for a time immortality.
And so the body marked
the intervening years
in front of the tv
upright on sticks of Ercol furniture
as my soul soared off
a canvas bag of broken springs
never to bounce back
far above the conspiring earth
that from a height
looked like a swirling
spiral patterned carpet
constantly repeating itself.

GROWING

In the old park
kicking up
horse chestnut leaves.
The palm of his hand.

www.ingramcontent.com/pod-product-compliance
Lightning Source LLC
Chambersburg PA
CBHW031437040426
42444CB00006B/851